# WESTERN

# BBQ

Publications International, Ltd.
www.pilcookbooks.com

**Pictured on the front cover:** Bodacious Grilled Ribs *(page 66).*
**Pictured on the back cover** *(top to bottom):* Chili-Rubbed Grilled Vegetable Kabobs *(page 92)* and Fresh Berry-Berry Cobbler *(page 110).*

ISBN-13: 978-0-7853-2146-0
ISBN-10: 0-7853-2146-2

Library of Congress Control Number: 2009933233

Manufactured in China.

8 7 6 5 4 3 2 1

**Microwave Cooking:** Microwave ovens vary in wattage. Use the cooking times as guidelines and check for doneness before adding more time.

**Preparation/Cooking Times:** Preparation times are based on the approximate amount of time required to assemble the recipe before cooking, baking, chilling or serving. These times include preparation steps such as measuring, chopping and mixing. The fact that some preparations and cooking can be done simultaneously is taken into account. Preparation of optional ingredients and serving suggestions is not included.

Publications International, Ltd.
**www.pilcookbooks.com**

# Table of Contents

Shoot 'Em Up Starters . . . . . . . . . . . 4

Calling All Cattle . . . . . . . . . . . . . . 20

Prize-Winning Pork . . . . . . . . . . . . . 46

Bird Bonanza. . . . . . . . . . . . . . . . . . 72

Grilling Sidekicks. . . . . . . . . . . . . . 92

Sassy Cowgirl Sweets. . . . . . . . . . . 108

Acknowledgments . . . . . . . . . . . . . 124

Index. . . . . . . . . . . . . . . . . . . . . . . 125

### Slow-Cooked Mini
### Pulled Pork Bites

1 can (10¾ ounces) CAMPBELL'S® Condensed Tomato Soup
½ cup packed brown sugar
¼ cup cider vinegar
1 teaspoon garlic powder
4 pounds boneless pork shoulder
1 package (13.9 ounces) PEPPERIDGE FARM® Soft Country Style
    Dinner Rolls
    Hot pepper sauce (optional)

**Slow Cooker Directions**

**1.** Stir the soup, brown sugar, vinegar and garlic powder in a 6-quart slow cooker. Add the pork and turn to coat.

**2.** Cover and cook on LOW for 6 to 7 hours* or until the pork is fork-tender.

**3.** Remove the pork from the cooker to a cutting board and let stand for 10 minutes. Using 2 forks, shred the pork. Return the pork to the cooker.

**4.** Divide the pork mixture among the rolls. Serve with the hot pepper sauce, if desired. *Makes 16 mini sandwiches*

*\*Or on HIGH for 4 to 5 hours.*

**Prep Time:** 10 minutes • **Cook Time:** 6 to 7 hours • **Stand Time:** 10 minutes

# Layered Beer Bean Dip

1 can (about 15 ounces) pinto beans, rinsed and drained
1 can (12 ounces) beer
1½ cups chopped onions
3 cloves garlic, minced
2 teaspoons ground cumin
1 teaspoon dried oregano
1 teaspoon salt
1 cup guacamole
1 cup sour cream
1 cup salsa
½ cup chopped black olives
½ cup chopped green onions
1½ cups (6 ounces) shredded Cheddar or Monterey Jack cheese
    Tortilla chips

**1.** Place beans in large saucepan over low heat. Add beer, onions, garlic, cumin, oregano and salt; cook and stir 15 to 30 minutes or until no liquid remains. Remove from heat. Mash beans with potato masher or process in food processor. Set aside to cool.

**2.** Spread half of cooled beans in 2-inch-deep dish. Top with half of guacamole, half of sour cream, half of salsa, half of olives and half of green onions. Repeat layers; top with cheese. Serve with tortilla chips.

*Makes 4 to 6 servings*

**Note:** This can be made the night before serving.

**Variation:** Use refried beans instead of whole beans. Pour a 15-ounce can of refried beans into a small saucepan. Add only 6 ounces of beer and simmer for about 10 minutes. If the refried beans are not seasoned, add garlic, cumin and oregano while simmering. Let cool and proceed.

# Tex-Mex Toasts

1 package (9.5 ounces) PEPPERIDGE FARM® Texas Toast
   Mozzarella Monterey Jack
6 tablespoons refried beans
   Sour cream
   Chopped green onion
   PACE® Chunky Salsa

**1.** Prepare the Texas Toast according to the package directions.

**2.** Spread **1 tablespoon** refried beans on **each** toast slice. Bake for 2 minutes or until the beans are hot.

**3.** Top the toast slices with the sour cream, green onion and salsa.

*Makes 6 servings*

**Prep Time:** 15 minutes • **Bake Time:** 10 minutes

# Chili con Queso

2 tablespoons butter
¼ cup finely chopped onion
1 clove garlic, minced
1 can (8 ounces) tomato sauce
1 can (4 ounces) diced green chiles, drained
2 cups (8 ounces) shredded Cheddar cheese
2 cups (8 ounces) shredded Monterey Jack cheese with jalapeño
   peppers
   Tortilla chips and crisp raw vegetable dippers

**1.** Melt butter in large saucepan over medium heat. Add onion and garlic; cook and stir until onion is tender. Stir in tomato sauce and chiles; reduce heat to low. Simmer 3 minutes. Gradually add cheeses, stirring until cheeses are melted and mixture is evenly blended.

**2.** Transfer to fondue pot or chafing dish; keep warm over heat source. Serve with tortilla chips and vegetable dippers.

*Makes 3 cups*

# Galveston Shrimp Salad

2 cups medium cooked shrimp, peeled and deveined
2 large tomatoes, peeled and diced
1 cucumber, peeled, seeded and diced
1 cup diced celery
1 can (4 ounces) chopped green chiles, drained
⅓ cup finely diced onion
2 tablespoons brown sugar
2 tablespoons vegetable oil
   Juice of 2 limes
1 jalapeño pepper,* seeded and minced
½ teaspoon salt
½ teaspoon celery seed
½ teaspoon black pepper
2 bay leaves
   Dash hot pepper sauce
6 to 8 red leaf lettuce leaves

*Jalapeño peppers can sting and irritate the skin, so wear rubber gloves when handling peppers and do not touch your eyes.*

Combine all ingredients except lettuce in large nonreactive bowl. Cover; refrigerate overnight. Remove and discard bay leaves. Stir salad. Serve on lettuce leaves.                                   *Makes 6 to 8 servings*

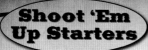
# Easy Taco Dip

½ pound ground beef
1 cup frozen corn
½ cup chopped onion
½ cup salsa
½ cup mild taco sauce
1 can (4 ounces) diced mild green chiles
1 can (4 ounces) sliced black olives, drained
1 cup (4 ounces) shredded Mexican cheese blend
Tortilla chips
Sour cream

**Slow Cooker Directions**

**1.** Brown ground beef 6 to 8 minutes in large skillet over medium-high heat, stirring to break up meat. Drain fat. Transfer beef to slow cooker.

**2.** Add corn, onion, salsa, taco sauce, chiles and olives to slow cooker; mix well. Cover; cook on LOW 2 to 3 hours.

**3.** Just before serving, stir in cheese. Serve with tortilla chips and sour cream. *Makes about 3 cups*

**Prep Time:** 15 minutes • **Cook Time:** 2 to 3 hours

**TIP**

To keep this dip hot through an entire party, simply leave it in the slow cooker on LOW.

★Easy Taco Dip★

# Rustic Texas-Que Pizza

2 cups shredded, cooked chicken (about 1 pound uncooked)
¼ cup *Frank's® RedHot®* Chile 'n Lime™ Hot Sauce or *Frank's®*
  *RedHot®* Buffalo Wing Sauce
1 pound prepared pizza or bread dough (thawed, if frozen)
1 cup *Cattlemen's®* Award Winning Classic Barbecue Sauce
2 ripe plum tomatoes, diced
½ cup finely diced red onion
½ cup sliced black olives (2.25-ounce can)
2 cups shredded taco blend cheese
  Cilantro or green onions, minced (optional)

**1.** Toss chicken with Chile 'n Lime™ Hot Sauce; set aside. Divide dough in
half. Gently stretch or roll each piece of dough into 13×9-inch rectangle
on floured surface. Coat one side with vegetable cooking spray.

**2.** Cook dough, coated side down, on greased grill over medium-high heat
for 5 minutes until browned and crisp on bottom. Using tongs, turn dough
over. Spread each pizza crust with barbecue sauce and top with chicken
mixture, tomatoes, onion, olives and cheese, dividing evenly.

**3.** Grill pizzas about 5 minutes longer until bottom is browned, crispy
and cheese melts. Garnish with minced cilantro or green onions, if
desired.                                          *Makes 8 servings*

**Variation:** Top pizza with different shredded cheeses, such as Cheddar
or Jack, or with other vegetables, such as whole kernel corn, jalapeño or
bell peppers.

**Tip:** For easier handling, allow pizza dough to rest 30 minutes in an oiled,
covered bowl at room temperature.

**Prep Time:** 15 minutes • **Cook Time:** 10 minutes

# Barbecue Chicken Sliders

　1 pound (16 ounces) ground chicken
　½ cup barbecue sauce, divided
　　Nonstick cooking spray
　4 slices sharp Cheddar cheese, quartered
　4 to 6 slices whole wheat sandwich bread
　　Lettuce leaves

**1.** Combine chicken and ¼ cup barbecue sauce in medium bowl. Shape mixture into 16 meatballs.

**2.** Spray large skillet or nonstick grill pan with cooking spray; heat over medium-high heat. Place meatballs in pan; press with spatula to make patties. Cook 6 minutes per side or until chicken is cooked through (165°F). Top with cheese.

**3.** Meanwhile, cut bread into circles or quarters; toast to desired doneness.

**4.** Top bread with remaining barbecue sauce, lettuce and burgers.

*Makes 16 burgers*

# Hot and Spicy Hummus Dip

　1 container (8 ounces) prepared hummus
　½ cup mayonnaise
　2 to 3 tablespoons chipotle salsa*
　1 tablespoon minced green onion
　　Pita chips and/or vegetables

*\*Chipotle salsa is a canned mixture of finely chopped chipotle peppers in adobo sauce. Look for it in the Latin foods section of the supermarket.*

**1.** Combine all ingredients except pita chips in medium bowl. Refrigerate until ready to serve.

**2.** Serve with pita chips.

*Makes about 6 servings*

**Serving Suggestion:** Use this spicy dip to liven up sandwiches or wraps.

**Prep Time:** 5 minutes

# Velveeta® Southwestern Corn Dip

1 pound (16 ounces) VELVEETA® Pasteurized Prepared Cheese
    Product, cut into ½-inch cubes
1 can (11 ounces) corn with red and green bell peppers, drained
3 jalapeño peppers, seeded, minced
1 red onion, finely chopped
½ cup fresh cilantro, finely chopped
½ cup BREAKSTONE'S® or KNUDSEN® Sour Cream

Mix VELVEETA® and corn in large microwaveable bowl. Microwave on
high 5 minutes or until VELVEETA® is completely melted, stirring after
3 minutes.

Stir in remaining ingredients.

Serve hot with WHEAT THINS® Snack Crackers or assorted cut-up fresh
vegetables.        *Makes 3½ cups or 28 servings, 2 tablespoons each.*

**To Halve:** Mix ingredients as directed in 1-quart microwaveable bowl,
cutting all ingredients in half. Microwave on high 3 to 4 minutes or until
VELVEETA® is completely melted, stirring after 2 minutes. Serve as
directed. Makes 1½ cups or 12 servings, 2 tablespoons each.

**Keeping It Safe:** Hot dips should be discarded after sitting at room
temperature for 2 hours or longer.

**How To Make It Spicy:** Save the seeds from one of the jalapeños
and add to the dip. Or if you like it really fiery, no need to seed the
peppers at all. Simply slice off the stems and chop.

**Prep Time:** 5 minutes • **Total Time:** 10 minutes

## Cavemen Beef Back Ribs

¼ cup paprika
¼ cup brown sugar
¼ cup seasoned salt
2 full racks beef back ribs, split in half (about 6 to 8 pounds)
1 cup *Cattlemen's*® Authentic Smoke House Barbecue Sauce
¼ cup apple, pineapple or orange juice

**1.** Combine paprika, sugar and seasoned salt. Rub mixture into ribs. Cover ribs and refrigerate 1 to 3 hours.

**2.** Prepare grill for indirect cooking over medium-low heat (250°F). Place ribs on rib rack or in foil pan. Cook on covered grill 2½ to 3 hours until very tender.

**3.** Meanwhile, combine barbecue sauce and juice. Brush mixture on ribs during last 30 minutes of cooking. Serve with additional barbecue sauce.

*Makes 6 to 8 servings*

**Tip:** For very tender ribs, remove membrane from underside of ribs before cooking. With a sharp paring knife, score membrane on bone from underside of ribs. Lift up portions of membrane with point of knife. Using kitchen towel, pull membrane away from bone and discard.

**Prep Time:** 5 minutes • **Cook Time:** 3 hours • **Marinate Time:** 1 hour

# Spicy Onion Steak Sandwiches

1 cup barbecue sauce
3 tablespoons chipotle salsa*
1 tablespoon vegetable oil
1 large onion, sliced
1 pound sandwich steaks,** cut into wide strips
4 sub rolls, split
8 slices sharp white Cheddar or Monterey Jack cheese

*Chipotle salsa is a canned mixture of finely chopped chipotle peppers in adobo sauce. Look for it in the Latin foods section of the supermarket.*

**You may substitute 1 pound thick-sliced deli roast beef for the sandwich steaks. Omit step 3.*

**1.** Combine barbecue sauce and chipotle salsa in small bowl. Reserve ½ cup mixture.

**2.** Heat oil in large nonstick skillet over medium heat. Add onion; cook and stir 10 minutes or until lightly browned. Add remaining barbecue sauce mixture; toss to combine. Remove from heat.

**3.** Heat nonstick grill pan over high heat. Cook steak strips 2 minutes on each side.

**4.** Brush reserved sauce evenly onto rolls. Divide onion, steak and cheese slices evenly among rolls.                    *Makes 4 servings*

★**Spicy Onion Steak Sandwich**★

# Texas Smoked BBQ Brisket

½ cup prepared barbecue seasoning

2 tablespoons ground chili powder

1 (5 to 7 pound) beef brisket, trimmed with a layer of fat (center flat portion)

1 cup *Frank's® RedHot®* Chile 'n Lime™ Hot Sauce or *Frank's® RedHot®* Cayenne Pepper Sauce

1½ cups beer or non-alcoholic malt beverage

1 cup *Cattlemen's®* Authentic Smoke House Barbecue Sauce or *Cattlemen's®* Award Winning Classic Barbecue Sauce

¼ cup butter

**1.** Combine barbecue seasoning and chili powder. Rub mixture thoroughly into beef. Place meat, fat-side up, into disposable foil pan. Cover and refrigerate 1 to 3 hours. Just before using, prepare mop sauce by combining Chile 'n Lime™ Hot Sauce and 1 cup beer; set aside.

**2.** Prepare grill for indirect cooking over medium-low heat (250°F). If desired, toss soaked wood chips over coals or heat source. Place pan with meat in center of grill over indirect heat. Cover grill. Cook meat over low heat 6 to 7 hours until meat is very tender (190°F internal temperature). Baste with mop sauce once an hour.

**3.** Combine barbecue sauce, butter and remaining ½ cup beer. Simmer 5 minutes until slightly thickened. Slice meat and serve with sauce.

*Makes 10 to 12 servings*

**Tip:** To easily slice meat, cut against the grain using an electric knife.

**Prep Time:** 15 minutes • **Cook Time:** 7 hours • **Marinate Time:** 1 hour

# Spicy Smoked Beef Ribs

Wood chunks or chips for smoking
4 to 6 pounds beef back ribs, cut into 3- to 4-rib pieces
Black pepper
1⅓ cups barbecue sauce
2 teaspoons hot pepper sauce or Szechwan chili sauce
Beer at room temperature or hot water

**1.** Soak 4 wood chunks or several handfuls of wood chips in water at least 30 minutes; drain.

**2.** Spread ribs on baking sheet or tray; season with black pepper. Combine barbecue sauce and hot pepper sauce in small bowl. Brush ribs with half of sauce. Marinate in refrigerator 30 minutes to 1 hour.

**3.** Prepare grill for indirect cooking. Add soaked wood to fire (if using chips, reserve some for adding during cooking). Place foil drip pan in center of grill; fill pan half full with beer.

**4.** Oil hot grid. Place ribs on grid, meaty side up, directly above drip pan. Grill ribs over low heat, covered, about 1 hour or until meat is fork-tender, brushing remaining sauce over ribs 2 or 3 times during cooking. (If grill has thermometer, maintain cooking temperature between 250°F to 275°F. Add a few more briquets as needed to maintain constant temperature. Add more soaked wood chips, if necessary.)          *Makes 4 to 6 servings*

# Campfire Hot Dogs

½ pound ground beef
2 cups RAGÚ® Old World Style® Pasta Sauce
1 can (10¾ to 16 ounces) baked beans
8 frankfurters, cooked
8 frankfurter rolls

**1.** In 12-inch skillet, brown ground beef over medium-high heat; drain.

**2.** Stir in Ragú Pasta Sauce and beans. Bring to a boil over high heat. Reduce heat to low and simmer, stirring occasionally, 5 minutes.

**3.** To serve, arrange frankfurters in rolls and top with sauce mixture. Garnish, if desired, with Cheddar cheese.          *Makes 8 servings*

**Tip:** For Chili Campfire Hot Dogs, simply stir 2 to 3 teaspoons chili powder into sauce mixture.

**Prep Time:** 5 minutes • **Cook Time:** 10 minutes

# Texas Meets N.Y. Strip Steaks

3 tablespoons olive oil, divided
2 medium onions, thinly sliced
4 strip steaks (6 to 8 ounces each)
2 teaspoons minced garlic
2 teaspoons black pepper

**1.** Heat 2 tablespoons oil in medium skillet over medium heat. Add onions; cook and stir 15 to 20 minutes or until soft and golden brown.

**2.** Meanwhile, rub steaks with remaining 1 tablespoon oil and garlic. Sprinkle pepper on both sides of steaks. Prepare grill for direct cooking.

**3.** Grill steaks over medium-high heat 10 to 12 minutes to at least 145°F or to desired degree of doneness, turning twice to obtain cross-hatch grill marks. Serve steaks topped with onions.          *Makes 4 servings*

# Grilled Skirt Steak Fajitas

1½ pounds skirt steak
½ cup pale ale
3 tablespoons lime juice
1 teaspoon ground cumin
2 tablespoons olive oil
1 cup thinly sliced red onion
1 cup thinly sliced red and green bell peppers
2 cloves garlic, minced
3 plum tomatoes, each cut into 4 wedges
1 tablespoon reduced-sodium soy sauce
¾ teaspoon salt
¼ teaspoon black pepper
8 (7-inch) flour tortillas
   Avocado slices, salsa and sour cream (optional)

**1.** Combine steak, pale ale, lime juice and cumin in resealable food storage bag; toss to coat. Refrigerate 2 hours, turning occasionally.

**2.** Meanwhile, heat oil in large nonstick skillet over medium-high heat. Add onion; cook and stir 2 to 3 minutes or until starting to soften. Add bell peppers; cook and stir 7 to 8 minutes or until softened. Add garlic; cook and stir 1 minute. Add tomatoes; cook 2 minutes or until just beginning to soften. Add soy sauce; cook 1 minute. Keep warm.

**3.** Prepare grill for direct cooking.

**4.** Lightly oil grid. Remove steak from marinade; discard marinade. Sprinkle with salt and pepper. Grill steak over medium-high heat 4 to 6 minutes on each side for medium-rare (145°F) or to desired degree of doneness. Transfer to cutting board; cut across grain into ¼-inch-thick slices.

**5.** To serve, warm tortillas and fill with steak and vegetable mixture. Top with avocado slices, salsa and sour cream, if desired.

*Makes 4 servings*

# Texas Chili

2 tablespoons vegetable oil
3½ pounds beef top round steak, ¾-inch thick, cut into ¼-inch
    pieces
3 medium onions, chopped (about 1½ cups)
2 medium green peppers, chopped (about 1 cup)
2 cloves garlic, minced or 1 teaspoon garlic powder
4 cups V8® Vegetable Juice
3 tablespoons chili powder
¼ teaspoon ground red pepper
1 can (14½ ounces) diced tomatoes

**1.** Heat **1 tablespoon** of the oil in 6-quart saucepot over medium-high
heat. Add the beef in 3 batches and cook until it's well browned. Remove
the beef with a slotted spoon and set aside. Pour off any fat.

**2.** Reduce the heat to medium and add the remaining oil. Add the onions,
green peppers and garlic. Cook and stir until the vegetables are tender-
crisp. Pour off any fat.

**3.** Add the vegetable juice, chili powder, red pepper and tomatoes. Heat to
a boil. Reduce the heat to low and return the beef to the saucepot. Cover
and cook for 1 hour and 45 minutes or until beef is fork-tender.

*Makes 8 servings*

**Hands On Time:** 30 minutes • **Cook Time:** 2 hours 10 minutes

**TIP**

A slow-cooked chili is a great place to use slightly
tougher cuts of meat, like round steak. Long,
moist cooking will help break down connective
tissue and make meat more tender.

★Texas Chili★

# All-American Onion Burger

1 pound ground beef
2 tablespoons *French's*® Worcestershire Sauce
1⅓ cups *French's*® French Fried Onions, divided
½ teaspoon garlic salt
¼ teaspoon ground black pepper
4 hamburger rolls

Combine beef, Worcestershire, ⅔ *cup* French Fried Onions, garlic salt and pepper. Form into 4 patties. Place patties on grid. Grill over hot coals about 10 minutes or until meat thermometer inserted into beef reaches 160°F, turning once. Top with remaining ⅔ *cup* onions. Serve on rolls.

*Makes 4 servings*

**Luscious Oniony Cheeseburger:** Place 1 slice cheese on each burger before topping with French Fried Onions.

**Tangy Western Burger:** Top each burger with 1 tablespoon barbecue sauce and 1 strip crisp bacon before topping with French Fried Onions.

**California Burger:** Combine 2 tablespoons each mayonnaise, sour cream and *French's*® Spicy Brown Mustard in small bowl; spoon over burgers. Top each burger with avocado slices, sprouts and French Fried Onions.

**Salisbury Steak Burger:** Prepare 1 package brown gravy mix according to directions. Stir in 1 can (4 ounces) drained sliced mushrooms. Spoon over burgers and top with French Fried Onions.

**Pizza Burger:** Top each burger with pizza sauce, mozzarella cheese and French Fried Onions.

**Chili Burger:** Combine 1 can (15 ounces) chili without beans, 2 tablespoons *Frank's*® *RedHot*® Sauce and 2 teaspoons each chili powder and ground cumin. Cook until heated through. Spoon over burgers and top with French Fried Onions.

**Prep Time:** 10 minutes • **Cook Time:** 10 minutes

★**California Burger**★

# Chipotle-Rubbed Flank Steak

1 packet (1.25 ounces) ORTEGA® Smokey Chipotle Taco
    Seasoning Mix, divided
½ cup water
¼ cup REGINA® Red Wine Vinegar
1½ to 2 pounds flank steak
  1 tablespoon olive oil
  1 small onion, diced
  1 tablespoon ORTEGA® Fire-Roasted Diced Green Chiles
  1 cup ORTEGA® Garden Salsa
    Juice from ½ lime

Combine one-half of seasoning mix, water and vinegar in shallow dish.
Add steak and turn to coat well. Marinate 15 minutes in refrigerator.
Turn over and marinate 15 minutes longer.

Heat oil in small saucepan over medium heat. Add onion; cook and stir
5 minutes or until translucent. Stir in chiles and salsa; cook and stir over
low heat 5 minutes.

Sprinkle remaining seasoning mix over both sides of steak. Broil or grill
steak over high heat 5 minutes on each side, or to desired doneness. Let
stand 5 minutes before slicing against grain. To serve, drizzle on sauce
and lime juice. *Makes 4 to 6 servings*

**Tip:** For a less formal meal, create flavorful tacos instead. Simply serve
the steak and sauce in soft tortillas, and garnish with shredded lettuce,
diced tomatoes and shredded cheese, if desired.

**Prep Time:** 10 minutes • **Start to Finish:** 1 hour

# BBQ Beef Sandwiches

1 boneless beef chuck roast (about 3 pounds)
¼ cup ketchup
2 tablespoons packed brown sugar
2 tablespoons red wine vinegar
1 tablespoon Dijon mustard
1 tablespoon Worcestershire sauce
1 clove garlic, minced
¼ teaspoon salt
¼ teaspoon liquid smoke (optional)
⅛ teaspoon black pepper
10 to 12 French rolls or sandwich buns

**Slow Cooker Directions**

**1.** Place beef in slow cooker. Combine remaining ingredients except rolls in medium bowl; pour over meat in slow cooker.

**2.** Cover; cook on LOW 8 to 9 hours or until meat is fork-tender.

**3.** Remove beef from slow cooker; shred with 2 forks. Combine beef with 1 cup sauce from slow cooker in large bowl. Serve meat mixture on warmed rolls.                    *Makes 10 to 12 servings*

These BBQ Beef Sandwiches make a great lunch the next day. Just keep the meat mixture separate from the rolls until ready to serve.

★BBQ Beef Sandwich★

# Tijuana T-Bones

1½ cups PACE® Chunky Salsa
2½ teaspoons ground cumin
 4 T-bone steaks (about 8 ounces each), ½-inch thick
 2 tablespoons fresh lime juice
 ¼ cup chopped fresh cilantro leaves
 1 can (about 15 ounces) black beans, rinsed and drained
 1 large avocado, peeled, pitted and chopped (about 1½ cups)

**1.** Stir **1 cup** of the salsa and **2 teaspoons** of the cumin in a 13×9×2-inch shallow, nonmetallic dish or gallon-size resealable plastic bag. Add the steaks and turn them over to coat with the marinade. Cover the dish or seal the plastic bag and refrigerate it for 1 hour, turning the steaks over a few times while they're marinating.

**2.** Stir the remaining salsa, remaining cumin, lime juice, cilantro, beans and avocado in a medium bowl and set aside.

**3.** Lightly oil the grill rack and heat the grill to medium. Remove the steaks from the marinade. Throw away any remaining marinade.

**4.** Grill the steaks for 12 minutes for medium-rare* or to desired doneness, turning the steaks over halfway through cooking. Serve the steaks with the salsa mixture.                     *Makes 4 servings*

*\*The internal temperature of the meat should reach 145°F.*

**Prep Time:** 10 minutes • **Marinate Time:** 1 hour • **Grill Time:** 12 minutes

★Tijuana T-Bone★

**Calling All Cattle**

# Bold and Zesty Beef Back Ribs

5 pounds beef back ribs, cut into 3- or 4-rib pieces
Salt and black pepper
1 teaspoon vegetable oil
1 small onion, minced
2 cloves garlic, minced
1 cup ketchup
½ cup chili sauce
2 tablespoons lemon juice
1 tablespoon packed brown sugar
1 teaspoon hot pepper sauce

**1.** Place ribs in shallow pan; season with salt and pepper. Refrigerate until ready to grill.

**2.** Prepare grill for indirect cooking.

**3.** Meanwhile, heat oil in large nonstick saucepan over medium heat. Add onion and garlic; cook and stir 5 minutes or until onion is tender. Stir in ketchup, chili sauce, lemon juice, brown sugar and hot pepper sauce. Reduce heat to medium-low; cook 15 minutes, stirring occasionally. Reserve half of sauce.

**4.** Place ribs on grid directly over drip pan. Grill over medium-low heat, covered, 45 to 60 minutes or until meat is fork-tender, turning occasionally and basting with remaining sauce.

**5.** Serve ribs with reserved sauce.        *Makes 5 to 6 servings*

**Prep Time:** 15 minutes • **Cook Time:** 1 hour 5 minutes to 1 hour 20 minutes

# Grilled T-Bone Steaks with BBQ Rub

2 to 4 well-trimmed beef T-Bone or Porterhouse steaks, cut
    1 inch thick (about 2 to 4 pounds)

**BBQ Rub:**
    2 tablespoons chili powder
    2 tablespoons packed brown sugar
    1 tablespoon ground cumin
    2 teaspoons minced garlic
    2 teaspoons cider vinegar
    1 teaspoon Worcestershire sauce
    ¼ teaspoon ground red pepper

**1.** Combine rub ingredients; press evenly onto beef steaks.

**2.** Place steak on grid over medium, ash-covered coals. Grill, covered
14 to 16 minutes (over medium heat on preheated gas grill, covered, 15 to
19 minutes) for medium rare doneness, turning occasionally. Season with
salt, as desired.                           *Makes 4 servings*

**Cook's Tip:** To broil, place steaks on rack in broiler pan so surface of
beef is 3 to 4 inches from heat. Broil 15 to 20 minutes for medium-rare to
medium doneness, turning once.

**Prep and Cook Time:** 25 minutes

Favorite recipe from *National Cattlemen's Beef Association*

# Smokin' Texas Chili

2 tablespoons olive oil

1½ pounds boneless beef sirloin steak or top round steak, ¾-inch
thick, cut into ½-inch pieces

1 medium onion, chopped (about ½ cup)

2 cloves garlic, minced

3 cups PACE® Chunky Salsa, any variety

½ cup water

1 tablespoon chili powder

1 teaspoon ground cumin

1 can (about 15 ounces) red kidney beans, rinsed and drained

¼ cup chopped fresh cilantro leaves

*Chili Toppings* (optional)

**1.** Heat **1 tablespoon** oil in a 6-quart saucepot over medium-high heat. Add the beef in 2 batches and cook until it's well browned, stirring often. Remove the beef from the saucepot.

**2.** Add the remaining oil and heat over medium heat. Add the onion and cook until it's tender. Add the garlic and cook for 30 seconds.

**3.** Add the salsa, water, chili powder and cumin. Heat to a boil. Return the beef to the saucepot. Stir in the beans. Reduce the heat to low. Cover and cook for 1 hour. Uncover and cook for 30 minutes or until the beef is fork-tender.

**4.** Sprinkle with the cilantro and Chili Toppings, if desired.

*Makes 6 servings*

**Chili Toppings:** Chopped tomatoes, chopped onions, sour cream **or** shredded cheese.

**Prep Time:** 15 minutes • **Cook Time:** 1 hour, 45 minutes

# Prize-Winning Pork

## Barbequed Ribs

1 cup ketchup
½ cup GRANDMA'S® Molasses
¼ cup cider vinegar
¼ cup Dijon mustard
2 tablespoons Worcestershire sauce
1 teaspoon garlic powder
1 teaspoon hickory flavor liquid smoke (optional)
¼ teaspoon ground red pepper
¼ teaspoon hot pepper sauce
4 to 6 pounds baby back ribs

**1.** Prepare grill for direct cooking. While coals are heating, combine all ingredients except ribs in large bowl; mix well. Place ribs on grid over medium-hot coals. Cook ribs 40 to 45 minutes or until they begin to brown, turning occasionally.

**2.** Once ribs begin to brown, begin basting them with sauce. Continue to cook and baste ribs with sauce an additional 1 to 1½ hours or until tender and cooked through.*                               *Makes 4 to 6 servings*

*Do not baste during last 5 minutes of grilling; discard remaining sauce.*

# Cowboy Coffee Chili

3 pounds boneless pork shoulder, trimmed and cut into
    1½-inch pieces
2 tablespoons all-purpose flour
2 tablespoons vegetable oil
1 onion, chopped
3 cloves garlic, minced
3½ cups enchilada sauce
2 cups strong brewed coffee
2 cans (about 15 ounces each) chili beans
2 cans (about 15 ounces each) pinto beans, rinsed and drained
    Sliced green onions, shredded Cheddar cheese and sour cream
    (optional)

**1.** Place pork and flour in large resealable food storage bag; shake to coat.

**2.** Heat oil in Dutch oven over medium-high heat. Working in batches, brown pork on all sides; remove to plate.

**3.** Add onion to Dutch oven; scrape up browned bits on bottom. Cook and stir onion until golden. Add garlic; cook and stir 30 seconds. Return pork and accumulated juices to Dutch oven. Stir in enchilada sauce and coffee. Reduce heat to medium-low; simmer, uncovered, 2 hours or until pork is tender.

**4.** Stir in chili and pinto beans; simmer 10 minutes. Serve chili with green onions, cheese and sour cream, if desired.          *Makes 6 servings*

# Enchilada Slow-Roasted Baby Back Ribs

**1 packet (1.25 ounces) ORTEGA® Fajita Seasoning Mix**
**4 tablespoons packed brown sugar**
**4 slabs baby back ribs (about 10 pounds)**
**½ cup Dijon mustard**
**2 jars (8 ounces each) ORTEGA® Enchilada Sauce**

Preheat oven to 250°F. Combine seasoning mix and brown sugar in small bowl. Place large piece of aluminum foil on counter. On foil, brush both sides of ribs with mustard; sprinkle both sides with seasoning mixture.

Adjust one oven rack to low position. Remove remaining oven rack; arrange ribs on rack. Slide rack with ribs into upper-middle position in oven. Place foil-lined baking sheet on lower rack to collect drippings from ribs.

Roast ribs 1½ to 2 hours or until tender. Remove ribs from oven. Turn on broiler.

Brush enchilada sauce onto both sides of ribs. Transfer ribs to foil-lined baking sheet, meat side down. Broil 5 to 6 minutes or until sauce begins to bubble. Let stand 5 minutes before slicing into individual servings.

*Makes 6 to 8 servings*

**Tip:** You can also grill the ribs. Follow the same procedures, keeping the grill temperature at about 250°F and grill with the cover on.

**Prep Time:** 15 minutes • **Start to Finish:** 2 hours

# Texas Barbecued Ribs

1 cup GRANDMA'S® Molasses
½ cup coarse-grained mustard
2 tablespoons cider vinegar
2 teaspoons dry mustard
3½ pounds pork loin baby back ribs or spareribs, cut into
     6 sections

Prepare grill for direct cooking. In medium bowl, combine molasses, coarse-grained mustard, cider vinegar and dry mustard. When ready to cook, place ribs on grill, meaty side up, over medium-hot coals. Grill 1 to 1¼ hours or until meat is tender and starts to pull away from bone, basting frequently with sauce* during last 15 minutes of grilling. To serve, cut ribs apart carefully with knife and arrange on platter.

*Makes 4 servings*

*Do not baste during last 5 minutes of cooking.*

## TIP

Purchase about 1 pound of ribs per person. It seems like a lot, but it ends up being about a half a slab per serving.

# Pork Tenderloin Sliders

2 teaspoons chili powder
¾ teaspoon ground cumin
½ teaspoon salt
½ teaspoon black pepper
2 tablespoons olive oil, divided
2 pork tenderloins (about 1 pound each)
12 green onions, ends trimmed
½ cup mayonnaise
1 chipotle pepper in adobo sauce, minced
2 teaspoons lime juice
12 dinner rolls, halved
12 slices Monterey Jack cheese

**1.** Prepare grill for direct cooking.

**2.** Combine chili powder, cumin, salt and black pepper in small bowl. Rub 1 tablespoon oil evenly over tenderloins. Sprinkle seasoning mixture evenly over tenderloins, coating all sides. Place green onions and remaining 1 tablespoon oil in large resealable food storage bag; seal bag. Knead to coat green onions with oil. Set aside.

**3.** Combine mayonnaise, chipotle pepper and lime juice is small bowl until well blended. Cover and refrigerate.

**4.** Grill tenderloins, covered, 15 to 20 minutes or until 160°F, turning occasionally. Remove to cutting board. Tent with foil; let stand 10 minutes.

**5.** Meanwhile, grill green onions about 3 minutes or until browned, turning frequently.

**6.** Coarsely chop green onions. Thinly slice tenderloins. Evenly spread chipotle mayonnaise on bottom halves of rolls. Top with green onions, tenderloin slices and cheese. Replace roll tops. Serve immediately.

*Makes 12 sandwiches*

# Sweet 'n' Sour Country Ribs

3 pounds country-style pork ribs, fat trimmed
3 large sweet potatoes, peeled and cut into 2-inch chunks
2 cups apple juice
¼ cup packed brown sugar
¼ cup cider vinegar
¼ cup *French's*® Worcestershire Sauce
2 tablespoons *French's*® Spicy Brown Mustard
2 tart green apples, cored and cut into 1-inch chunks
1 tablespoon cornstarch

**1.** Heat 1 tablespoon oil in 6-quart saucepot or Dutch oven over high heat. Cook ribs 10 minutes or until well browned on all sides; drain fat.

**2.** Add potatoes to ribs. Whisk together apple juice, sugar, vinegar, Worcestershire and mustard. Pour over rib mixture; stir well. Heat to boiling. Reduce heat to low. Cook, covered, 40 minutes or until pork is tender and no longer pink in center, stirring occasionally.

**3.** Stir in apples; cook 5 minutes or until tender. Transfer ribs, potatoes and apples to platter; keep warm. Combine cornstarch with 2 tablespoons water. Stir into pot. Heat to boiling, whisking constantly. Cook 1 to 2 minutes or until liquid thickens, stirring often. Serve with corn and crusty bread, if desired.          *Makes 6 servings (with 2 cups gravy)*

**20 Minute Marinade:** Marinate 1 pound steak, chicken or chops for 20 minutes in ¼ cup *French's*® Worcestershire Sauce.

**Prep Time:** 10 minutes • **Cook Time:** about 1 hour

# Puerco Sabrosas (Savory Pork)

3 tablespoons vegetable oil
1½ pounds lean pork, cut into 1×1½-inch strips
    Salt
    Black pepper
1 green bell pepper, finely chopped
1 medium onion, finely chopped
2 green chiles* (Hatch or Anaheim), seeded and minced
1 clove garlic, minced
1 can (about 14 ounces) whole stewed tomatoes, crushed
2 tablespoons chopped fresh cilantro
1 teaspoon chopped fresh oregano
1 teaspoon ground cumin
    Beer or water (optional)
    Hot cooked rice

*Chiles can sting and irritate the skin, so wear rubber gloves when handling peppers and do not touch your eyes.*

**1.** Preheat oven to 350°F.

**2.** Heat oil in ovenproof Dutch oven or large ovenproof skillet over medium-high heat. Add pork; cook and stir 5 to 6 minutes or until browned on both sides. Season with salt and black pepper.

**3.** Add bell pepper, onion, chiles and garlic to Dutch oven; cook and stir until onion and peppers are tender.

**4.** Add tomatoes, cilantro, oregano and cumin; mix well. Bake, covered, 30 minutes; stir well. Add beer or water, if needed. Continue cooking about 1½ hours or until pork is fork-tender. Serve over rice.

*Makes 6 servings*

# Rio Grande Ribs

4 pounds country-style pork ribs, trimmed of all visible fat
Salt, to taste
Black pepper, to taste
1 jar (16 ounces) picante sauce
½ cup beer, nonalcoholic malt beverage or beef broth
¼ cup *Frank's® RedHot®* Cayenne Pepper Sauce
1 teaspoon chili powder
2 cups *French's®* French Fried Onions

**Slow Cooker Directions**

**1.** Season ribs with salt and pepper. Broil ribs 6 inches from heat on rack in broiler pan for 10 minutes or until well-browned, turning once. Place ribs in slow cooker. Combine picante sauce, beer, *Frank's® RedHot®* Cayenne Pepper Sauce and chili powder in small bowl. Pour mixture over top.

**2.** Cover and cook on LOW for 6 hours or on HIGH for 3 hours or until ribs are tender. Transfer ribs to serving platter; keep warm. Skim fat from liquid.

**3.** Turn slow cooker to HIGH. Add 1 cup *French's®* French Fried Onions to the stoneware. Cook 10 to 15 minutes or until slightly thickened. Spoon sauce over ribs and sprinkle with remaining 1 cup French Fried Onions. Splash on more *Frank's® RedHot®* Cayenne Pepper Sauce to taste.

*Makes 6 servings*

# Pulled Pork Sandwiches

2 tablespoons kosher salt

2 tablespoons packed light brown sugar

2 tablespoons paprika

1 teaspoon dry mustard

1 teaspoon black pepper

1 boneless pork shoulder roast (about 3 pounds)

1½ cups stout

½ cup cider vinegar

6 to 8 large hamburger buns, split

¾ cup barbecue sauce

**1.** Preheat oven to 325°F. Combine salt, sugar, paprika, dry mustard and pepper in small bowl; mix well. Rub into pork.

**2.** Place pork in ovenproof Dutch oven. Add stout and vinegar. Cover; bake 3 hours or until pork is fork-tender. Cool 15 to 30 minutes or until cool enough to handle.

**3.** Shred pork into large pieces using 2 forks. Divide onto buns and serve warm with barbecue sauce.                    *Makes 6 to 8 servings*

**Tip:** This recipe is a great dish for a summer or fall picnic or party. Baked beans, corn on the cob and watermelon are wonderful accompaniments.

## Classic Baby Back Ribs

3 to 4 pounds pork baby back ribs, cut into 3-rib portions (2 to
  3 racks)
1 cup *Cattlemen's*® Award Winning Classic Barbecue Sauce

**1.** Grill ribs over indirect heat on a covered grill for 1½ hours (or in a
350°F oven).

**2.** Baste with barbecue sauce. Cook 30 minutes longer until meat is very
tender. Serve with additional barbecue sauce.

*Makes about 4 servings*

**Prep Time:** 5 minutes • **Cook Time:** 2 hours

## Pork Paint

½ cup diced onion
½ cup (1 stick) butter
½ cup cider vinegar
½ cup lemon juice
½ cup Worcestershire sauce
¼ cup brown sugar
3 tablespoons sweet paprika
2 teaspoons dry hot mustard
1 to 2 teaspoons ground red pepper
  Hot pepper sauce to taste

Mix all ingredients in medium saucepan over medium-low heat; simmer
20 to 30 minutes. *Makes 3 cups*

**Note:** This spicy "mop"—a basting sauce that is swabbed onto the meat
with a mop or brush—is designed for long cooking with large cuts of pork
such as the shoulder. It gives the finished product a lovely color. Reserve a
portion for dipping at the table.

# Bodacious Grilled Ribs

2 tablespoons paprika
2 teaspoons dried basil
½ teaspoon onion powder
¼ teaspoon garlic powder
¼ teaspoon ground red pepper
¼ teaspoon black pepper
4 pounds pork loin back ribs, cut into 4- to 6-rib pieces
2 sheets (24×18 inches) heavy-duty foil, lightly sprayed with
   nonstick cooking spray
8 ice cubes
1 cup barbecue sauce
½ cup apricot fruit spread

**1.** Prepare grill for direct cooking.

**2.** Combine paprika, basil, onion powder, garlic powder, red pepper and black pepper in small bowl. Rub on both sides of rib pieces. Place 2 pounds of ribs in single layer in center of each foil sheet. Place 4 ice cubes in each packet.

**3.** Double-fold sides and ends of foil to seal packets, leaving head space for heat circulation.

**4.** Transfer packets to grid. Grill over medium coals, covered, 45 to 60 minutes or until tender.

**5.** Combine barbecue sauce and fruit spread in small bowl. Carefully open one end of each packet to allow steam to escape. Transfer ribs to grid. Brush with barbecue sauce mixture. Grill 5 to 10 minutes, brushing with sauce and turning often. *Makes 4 servings*

# Rough-Cut Smoky Red Pork

1 pork shoulder roast (about 4 pounds)
1 can (about 14 ounces) stewed tomatoes, drained
1 can (6 ounces) tomato paste with basil, oregano and garlic
1 cup chopped red bell pepper
2 to 3 canned chipotle peppers in adobo sauce, finely chopped and mashed with fork*
1 teaspoon salt
1½ to 2 tablespoons sugar

*For less heat, remove seeds from chipotle peppers before mashing.*

### Slow Cooker Directions

**1.** Coat slow cooker with nonstick cooking spray. Place pork, fat side up, in bottom. Combine tomatoes, tomato paste, bell pepper, chipotle peppers and salt in medium bowl. Pour over pork.

**2.** Cover; cook on HIGH 5 hours. Scrape tomato mixture into cooking liquid. Transfer pork to cutting board; let stand 15 minutes. Stir sugar into cooking liquid. Cook, uncovered, on HIGH 15 minutes.

**3.** To serve, remove fat from pork and slice. Pour sauce over pork slices.

*Makes 8 servings*

**Prep Time:** 10 minutes • **Cook Time:** 5¼ hours

# Spicy Baby Back Ribs

¼ cup packed brown sugar
2 teaspoons dry mustard
2 teaspoons seasoned salt
1 teaspoon garlic powder
1 teaspoon black pepper
2 tablespoons olive oil
2 racks pork baby back ribs (3½ to 4 pounds)
⅓ to ½ cup barbecue sauce, plus additional for serving
½ teaspoon hot pepper sauce

**1.** Prepare grill for indirect cooking.

**2.** Combine brown sugar, mustard, salt, garlic powder and black pepper in small bowl. Rub 1 tablespoon oil over each rack of ribs. Rub brown sugar mixture evenly over ribs.

**3.** Place ribs on grid directly over drip pan. Grill over medium coals, covered, 1 hour, turning occasionally.

**4.** Combine barbecue sauce and hot pepper sauce in small bowl. Baste ribs generously with sauce; grill 30 minutes or until ribs are tender, turning and basting with sauce occasionally.

**5.** Serve ribs with additional barbecue sauce for dipping.

*Makes 4 servings*

# Bird Bonanza

## Cumin BBQ Chicken

- 1 cup barbecue sauce
- ½ cup orange juice
- 3 tablespoons vegetable oil
- 2 tablespoons minced garlic
- 2 teaspoons ground coriander
- 2 teaspoons ground cumin
- 1 teaspoon black pepper
- ½ teaspoon salt
- 2 whole chickens (about 3½ pounds each), cut up

**1.** Prepare grill for direct cooking. Combine barbecue sauce, orange juice, oil, garlic, coriander, cumin, pepper and salt in medium bowl; mix well. Reserve ¾ cup sauce.

**2.** Grill chicken over medium heat, covered, 20 minutes, turning once. Brush lightly with remaining sauce. Grill about 20 minutes more or until chicken is cooked through (165°F).

**3.** Serve with reserved sauce.                    *Makes 8 servings*

**Oven Method:** Preheat oven to 375°F. Place chicken in foil-lined large shallow roasting pan. Prepare sauce; reserve ¾ cup. Brush chicken with remaining sauce. Bake 45 to 50 minutes or until chicken is cooked through (165°F). Baste chicken with sauce every 15 minutes. *Do not baste during last 5 minutes of baking.* Discard any remaining basting sauce. Serve with reserved sauce.

# Garlicky Gilroy Chicken Wings

2 pounds chicken wings
2 heads fresh garlic, separated into cloves and peeled*
1 cup olive oil
1 teaspoon hot pepper sauce, or to taste
1 cup grated Parmesan cheese
1 cup Italian-style dry bread crumbs
1 teaspoon black pepper
   Carrot and celery slices (optional)

*To peel whole heads of garlic, drop garlic heads into boiling water for 5 to 10 seconds. Immediately remove garlic with slotted spoon. Plunge garlic into cold water; drain. Peel away skins.*

**1.** Preheat oven to 375°F. Spray baking sheet with nonstick cooking spray.

**2.** Remove and discard wing tips. Cut each wing in half at joint.

**3.** Place garlic, oil and hot pepper sauce in food processor; process until smooth. Pour garlic mixture into small bowl. Combine cheese, bread crumbs and black pepper in shallow dish. Dip wings, 1 at a time, into garlic mixture, then roll in crumb mixture, coating evenly and shaking off excess.

**4.** Arrange wings in single layer on prepared baking sheet. Drizzle remaining garlic mixture over wings; sprinkle with remaining crumb mixture. Bake 45 to 60 minutes or until wings are cooked through, browned and crisp. Serve with carrot and celery slices, if desired.

*Makes about 6 servings*

# Chicken with Grilled Pineapple Salsa

1¼ cups WISH-BONE® Italian Dressing or Robusto Italian Dressing
¼ cup firmly packed dark brown sugar
¼ cup PLUS 2 tablespoons chopped fresh cilantro
2 pounds chicken thighs
2 tablespoons orange juice
¼ teaspoon salt
⅛ teaspoon ground red pepper
1 medium pineapple, peeled and cut into ¾-inch-thick slices
1 large red onion, cut into ½-inch-thick slices

**1.** Blend Wish-Bone Italian Dressing, sugar and ¼ cup cilantro for marinade. Pour ¾ cup marinade over chicken in large, shallow nonaluminum baking dish or plastic bag; turn to coat. Cover, or close bag, and marinate in refrigerator, turning occasionally, 3 to 24 hours. Refrigerate remaining marinade.

**2.** Combine 2 tablespoons refrigerated marinade, remaining 2 tablespoons cilantro, orange juice, salt and pepper in medium bowl for salsa; set aside.

**3.** Remove chicken from marinade, discarding marinade. Grill or broil chicken, pineapple and onion, turning once and brushing frequently with remaining refrigerated marinade. Grill until pineapple and onion are tender and chicken is thoroughly cooked. Chop pineapple and onion and toss with salsa mixture. Serve salsa with chicken. *Makes 4 servings*

**Prep Time:** 10 minutes • **Marinate Time:** 3 hours • **Cook Time:** 30 minutes

# Grilled Chicken with Chili Beer Baste

2 tablespoons vegetable oil
1 small onion, chopped
1 clove garlic, minced
½ cup ketchup
2 tablespoons brown sugar
2 teaspoons chili powder
2 chipotle peppers in adobo sauce, minced
1 teaspoon dry mustard
½ teaspoon salt
½ teaspoon black pepper
3 bottles (12 ounces each) pilsner beer
½ cup tomato juice
¼ cup Worcestershire sauce
1 tablespoon lemon juice
2 whole chickens (about 3½ pounds each), cut up

**1.** To make Chili Beer Baste, heat oil in large saucepan over medium heat. Add onion and garlic; cook and stir until onion is tender. Combine ketchup, brown sugar, chili powder, chipotle peppers, mustard, salt and black pepper in medium bowl. Add 1 bottle beer, tomato juice, Worcestershire sauce and lemon juice; whisk until well blended. Pour mixture into saucepan with onion and garlic. Bring to a simmer; cook until sauce is thickened slightly and reduced to about 2 cups. Let cool. Refrigerate overnight.

**2.** Place chicken pieces in 2 large resealable food storage bags. Pour remaining 2 bottles beer over chicken in both bags; seal bags. Refrigerate 8 hours or overnight.

**3.** Prepare grill for direct cooking. Remove chicken from beer; discard beer. Grill chicken over medium heat 15 to 20 minutes, turning occasionally.

**4.** Remove Chili Beer Baste from refrigerator; set aside 1 cup. Continue grilling chicken, basting frequently, 10 minutes or until cooked through (165°F). Warm reserved Chili Beer Baste and serve with chicken.

*Makes 8 servings*

# Shredded BBQ Chicken Sandwiches

1 jar (1 pound 10 ounces) RAGÚ® Old World Style® Pasta Sauce
3 tablespoons firmly packed brown sugar
2 tablespoons apple cider vinegar
1½ tablespoons chili powder
2 teaspoons garlic powder
1½ teaspoons onion powder
4 boneless, skinless chicken breast halves (about 1¼ pounds)
6 hamburger buns or round rolls

**1.** In 6-quart saucepot, cook Ragú Pasta Sauce, brown sugar, vinegar, chili powder, garlic powder and onion powder over medium heat, stirring occasionally, 5 minutes.

**2.** Season chicken, if desired, with salt and ground black pepper. Add chicken to sauce. Reduce heat to medium-low and simmer, covered, stirring occasionally, 20 minutes or until chicken is no longer pink in center. Remove saucepot from heat.

**3.** Remove chicken from sauce. Using two forks, shred chicken. Return shredded chicken to sauce and heat through. To serve, arrange chicken mixture on buns and garnish, if desired, with shredded Cheddar cheese.

*Makes 6 servings*

**Prep Time:** 5 minutes • **Cook Time:** 30 minutes

# Grilled Chicken with Southern Barbecue Sauce

1 tablespoon vegetable oil
½ cup chopped onion (about 1 small)
4 cloves garlic, minced
1 can (16 ounces) tomato sauce
¾ cup water
3 tablespoons packed light brown sugar
3 tablespoons chili sauce
2 teaspoons chili powder
2 teaspoons dried thyme
2 teaspoons Worcestershire sauce
¾ teaspoon ground red pepper
½ teaspoon ground cinnamon
½ teaspoon black pepper
6 skinless bone-in chicken breasts

**1.** Heat oil in medium nonstick skillet over medium heat. Add onion and garlic; cook and stir about 5 minutes or until tender.

**2.** Stir in tomato sauce, water, brown sugar, chili sauce, chili powder, thyme, Worcestershire sauce, red pepper, cinnamon and black pepper; bring to a boil. Reduce heat to low and simmer, uncovered, 30 minutes or until mixture is reduced to about 1½ cups. Reserve ¾ cup sauce for basting. Meanwhile, prepare grill for indirect cooking.

**3.** Grill chicken over medium heat, covered, 40 to 45 minutes or until cooked through (165°F), turning chicken several times and basting occasionally with reserved sauce.

**4.** Heat remaining sauce in skillet over medium heat; serve with chicken.

*Makes 6 servings*

# Grilled Chipotle Chicken Sandwiches

1 medium lime, halved
4 boneless skinless chicken breasts, flattened slightly
½ cup sour cream
2 tablespoons mayonnaise
1 canned chipotle pepper packed in adobo sauce
2 teaspoons adobo sauce from canned chipotle
⅛ teaspoon salt
   Black pepper
2 slices Swiss cheese, cut in half diagonally
4 whole wheat hamburger buns, split
4 leaves romaine lettuce
4 thin slices red onion

**1.** Squeeze juice from half of lime evenly over chicken. Coat grill grid with nonstick cooking spray; prepare grill for direct cooking.

**2.** Combine sour cream, mayonnaise, chipotle pepper, adobo sauce and salt in blender. Blend until smooth.

**3.** Grill chicken over medium-high heat 10 minutes. Turn and sprinkle with black pepper. Grill 10 minutes longer or until chicken is no longer pink in center. Move chicken to side of grill. Squeeze remaining lime half over chicken; top with cheese.

**4.** Place buns on grill; toast lightly. Spread with chipotle mixture. Fill with lettuce, chicken and onion. *Makes 4 servings*

# Chicken Wings in Cerveza

1½ pounds chicken wings or drumettes
1 teaspoon salt
1 teaspoon dried thyme
⅛ teaspoon black pepper
1 bottle (12 ounces) Mexican beer

**1.** Cut off and discard wing tips. Cut each wing in half at joint. Place chicken in shallow bowl; sprinkle with salt, thyme and pepper. Pour beer over chicken; toss to coat. Cover and refrigerate 2 to 6 hours.

**2.** Preheat oven to 375°F. Line baking sheet with foil; spray with nonstick cooking spray.

**3.** Drain chicken, reserving marinade. Arrange chicken on prepared baking sheet in single layer. Bake 40 minutes or until chicken is cooked through, turning and basting with reserved marinade occasionally. *Do not brush with marinade during last 5 minutes of baking.* Discard remaining marinade. Serve warm or at room temperature.      *Makes 6 servings*

**Note:** When using drumettes, simply place them in the marinade without cutting.

# Grilled Picante BBQ Chicken

¾ cup PACE® Picante Sauce
¼ cup barbecue sauce
6 skinless, boneless chicken breast halves

**1.** Stir the picante sauce and barbecue sauce in a small bowl. Reserve ½ **cup** picante sauce mixture for grilling. Set aside remaining picante sauce mixture to serve with the chicken.

**2.** Lightly oil the grill rack and heat the grill to medium. Grill the chicken for 15 minutes or until it's cooked through, turning and brushing often with the reserved picante sauce mixture during grilling. Discard any remaining picante sauce mixture.

**3.** Serve the chicken with the remaining ½ **cup** picante sauce mixture.
*Makes 6 servings*

**Tip:** This simple basting sauce also makes a zesty dipping sauce for chicken wings or nuggets.

**Prep Time:** 5 minutes • **Cook Time:** 15 minutes

# Pulled Turkey Sandwiches

1 tablespoon vegetable oil
1 small red onion, chopped
1 stalk celery, trimmed and chopped
3 cups coarsely chopped cooked turkey thigh meat
1 can (8 ounces) tomato sauce
¼ cup ketchup
2 tablespoons packed brown sugar
1 tablespoon cider vinegar
2 teaspoons Worcestershire sauce
1 teaspoon Dijon mustard
¼ teaspoon chipotle chili powder
⅛ teaspoon salt
4 hamburger buns

**1.** Heat oil in Dutch oven or deep skillet over medium-high heat. Add onion and celery; cook and stir 5 minutes or until tender.

**2.** Stir in turkey, tomato sauce, ketchup, brown sugar, cider vinegar, Worcestershire sauce, mustard, chili powder and salt.

**3.** Cover and simmer 45 minutes to 1 hour or until turkey is fork-tender. Shred with 2 forks. Serve turkey in buns.          *Makes 4 sandwiches*

**Tip:** The pulled turkey filling for these sandwiches freezes very well. Try doubling the recipe and freezing any leftovers. Before serving, simply thaw the filling in the refrigerator and reheat in the microwave.

★Pulled Turkey Sandwich★

# Santa Fe BBQ Ranch Salad

1 cup *Cattlemen's*® Golden Honey Barbecue Sauce, divided
½ cup ranch salad dressing
1 pound boneless, skinless chicken
12 cups washed and torn Romaine lettuce
1 small red onion, thinly sliced
1 small ripe avocado, diced ½-inch
4 ripe plum tomatoes, sliced
2 cups shredded Monterey Jack cheese
½ cup cooked, crumbled bacon

**1.** Prepare BBQ Ranch Dressing: Combine ½ cup barbecue sauce and salad dressing in small bowl; reserve.

**2.** Grill or broil chicken over medium-high heat 10 minutes until no longer pink in center. Cut into strips and toss with remaining ½ cup barbecue sauce.

**3.** Toss lettuce, onion, avocado, tomatoes, cheese and bacon in large bowl. Portion on salad plates, dividing evenly. Top with chicken and serve with BBQ Ranch Dressing. *Makes 4 servings*

**Tip:** Serve *Cattlemen's*® Golden Honey Barbecue Sauce as a dipping sauce with chicken nuggets or seafood kabobs.

**Prep Time:** 15 minutes • **Cook Time:** 10 minutes

## TIP

Chicken breasts or thighs may be used in this salad. Breast meat is lighter and milder in flavor, whereas thigh meat is darker and richer. Breasts are more expensive, so choose thighs for a more economical meal.

## Chili-Rubbed Grilled Vegetable Kabobs

2 ears corn, husked
1 medium sweet or red onion, cut into 12 wedges
1 red bell pepper, cut into 12 (1-inch) chunks
1 yellow bell pepper, cut into 12 (1-inch) chunks
1 green bell pepper, cut into 12 (1-inch) chunks
2 tablespoons olive oil
1 teaspoon seasoned salt
1 teaspoon chili powder
½ teaspoon sugar

**1.** Cut cobs crosswise into 1-inch pieces with large chef's knife. Alternately thread corn, onion and bell peppers onto 12-inch metal skewers. Brush oil evenly over vegetables. Combine seasoned salt, chili powder and sugar in small bowl; sprinkle over all sides of vegetables. Wrap skewers in heavy-duty foil; refrigerate up to 8 hours.

**2.** Prepare grill for direct cooking. Unwrap skewers; place on grid over medium heat. Grill 10 to 12 minutes or until vegetables are tender, turning occasionally.                    *Makes 4 servings*

# Super-Moist Cornbread

1 can (11 ounces) Mexican-style corn, drained
1 package (8½ ounces) corn muffin mix
½ cup HELLMANN'S® or BEST FOODS® Real Mayonnaise
1 egg, slightly beaten

**1.** Preheat oven to 400°F. Spray 8-inch round cake pan with nonstick cooking spray; set aside.

**2.** In medium bowl, combine all ingredients until moistened. Evenly spread in prepared pan.

**3.** Bake 25 minutes or until toothpick inserted into center comes out clean.                    *Makes 8 servings*

**Prep Time:** 5 minutes • **Cook Time:** 25 minutes

# Spicy Sausage Mac & Cheese Bake

3 hot Italian sausage links (about 1 pound)
¼ cup water
1 package (14 ounces) deluxe macaroni and cheese dinner
  Black pepper
1½ cups (6 ounces) shredded sharp Cheddar cheese

**1.** Preheat oven to 350°F. Spray 2-quart baking dish with nonstick cooking spray.

**2.** Place sausages and water in medium nonstick skillet over medium heat; cover and simmer 10 to 12 minutes. Remove cover; brown sausages on all sides. Remove from heat; cool slightly. Cut sausages in half lengthwise and then into ½-inch pieces.

**3.** Prepare macaroni and cheese according to package directions. Stir in sausage pieces. Season with pepper.

**4.** Spoon half of macaroni mixture into prepared baking dish. Sprinkle with ¾ cup cheese. Top with remaining half of macaroni mixture and remaining ¾ cup cheese. Bake 10 to 12 minutes or until heated through.
*Makes 4 to 6 servings*

# Best 'Cue Coleslaw

⅓ cup dill pickle relish
⅓ cup vegetable oil
3 tablespoons lime juice
2 tablespoons honey
1 teaspoon salt
1 teaspoon ground cumin
1 teaspoon ground red pepper
1 teaspoon black pepper
1 small head green cabbage, very thinly sliced
2 large carrots, shredded
1 bunch green onions, sliced
5 radishes, sliced

**1.** Combine relish, oil, lime juice, honey, salt, cumin, ground red pepper and black pepper in large bowl.

**2.** Add cabbage, carrots, green onions and radishes; stir until well combined. Chill at least 1 hour before serving.     *Makes 6 to 8 servings*

## TIP

Coleslaw can be made hundreds of different ways. Try experimenting with other veggies or even fruit, such as bell peppers, celery, apples or pears, in addition to the cabbage. You can even add sliced almonds or crumbled crisp-cooked bacon for a fun and crunchy twist.

★**Best 'Cue Coleslaw**★

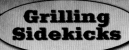

# Charred Corn Salad

  3 tablespoons lime juice
½ teaspoon salt
¼ cup extra-virgin olive oil
  4 to 6 ears corn, husked (enough to make 3 to 4 cups kernels)
⅔ cup canned black beans, rinsed and drained
½ cup chopped fresh cilantro
  2 teaspoons minced seeded chipotle pepper (1 canned
      chipotle pepper in adobo sauce or 1 dried chipotle pepper,
      reconstituted in boiling water)*

*Chipotle peppers can sting and irritate the skin, so wear rubber gloves when handling peppers and do not touch your eyes.*

**1.** Whisk lime juice, salt and oil in small bowl. Set aside.

**2.** Heat large grill pan or skillet over medium-high heat. Cook corn in single layer 15 to 17 minutes or until browned and tender, turning frequently. Transfer to plate to cool. Slice kernels off ears and place in medium bowl.

**3.** Microwave beans in small microwaveable bowl 1 minute or until heated through. Add beans, cilantro and chipotle pepper to corn; mix well. Pour lime juice mixture over corn mixture; toss to combine. Serve warm.                                         *Makes 6 servings*

**Note:** Chipotle peppers in adobo sauce are available canned in the Mexican food section of most supermarkets. Since only a small amount is needed for this dish, spoon leftovers into a covered plastic container and refrigerate or freeze.

★Charred Corn Salad★

# Salsa-Buttered Corn on the Cob

6 ears fresh corn, shucked
4 tablespoons butter, softened
¼ cup ORTEGA® Salsa
2 tablespoons ORTEGA® Taco Seasoning Mix, or to taste

Bring large pot of water to a boil. Add corn; cook 5 to 10 minutes.

Combine butter and salsa in small bowl; mix well. Place seasoning mix in another small bowl. Spread salsa butter onto cooked corn and sprinkle on seasoning mix to taste. *Makes 6 servings*

**Tip:** For a different side dish, cut the corn off the cob and heat in a skillet with the salsa butter and taco seasoning mix.

**Prep Time:** 5 minutes • **Start to Finish:** 20 minutes

# Sausage and Cheddar Cornbread

1 tablespoon vegetable oil
½ pound bulk pork sausage
1 medium onion, diced
1 jalapeño pepper,* diced
1 package (8 ounces) corn muffin mix
⅓ cup milk
1 egg
1 cup (4 ounces) shredded Cheddar cheese, divided

*Jalapeño peppers can sting and irritate the skin, so wear rubber gloves when handling peppers and do not touch your eyes.*

**1.** Heat oil in 10-inch cast iron skillet over medium heat. Brown sausage 6 minutes, stirring to break up meat. Add onion and jalapeño pepper; cook and stir 5 minutes or until vegetables are softened. Remove sausage mixture to medium bowl.

**2.** Preheat oven to 350°F. Combine corn muffin mix, milk, egg and ½ cup cheese in separate medium bowl. Pour batter into same skillet. Spread sausage mixture over top. Sprinkle with remaining ½ cup cheese.

**3.** Bake 20 to 25 minutes or until edges are lightly browned. Cut into wedges. Refrigerate leftovers. *Makes 10 servings*

★**Salsa-Buttered Corn on the Cob**★

# Mama's Best Baked Beans

1 bag (1 pound) dried Great Northern beans
1 package (1 pound) bacon
5 hot dogs, cut into ½-inch pieces
1 cup chopped onion
1 bottle (24 ounces) ketchup
2 cups dark brown sugar

**Slow Cooker Directions**

**1.** Soak and cook beans according to package directions. Drain and refrigerate until ready to use.

**2.** Cook bacon in skillet over medium-high heat until crisp. Drain on paper towels. Crumble bacon and set aside. Discard all but 3 tablespoons bacon fat from skillet. Add hot dogs and onion; cook and stir over medium heat until onion is tender. Combine cooked beans, bacon, hot dog mixture, ketchup and brown sugar in slow cooker. Cover; cook on LOW 2 to 4 hours. *Makes 4 servings*

# Santa Fe Salad

2 cups cooked brown rice, cooled
1 can (16 ounces) black beans or pinto beans, rinsed and drained
1 can (15 ounces) whole kernel corn, drained
¼ cup minced onion
¼ cup white vinegar
2 tablespoons vegetable oil
2 tablespoons snipped cilantro
2 jalapeño peppers,* minced
2 teaspoons chili powder
1 teaspoon salt

*\*Jalapeño peppers can sting and irritate the skin, so wear rubber gloves when handling peppers and do not touch your eyes.*

Combine rice, beans, corn and onion in medium bowl. Combine vinegar, oil, cilantro, peppers, chili powder and salt in small jar with lid. Pour over rice mixture; toss lightly. Cover and chill 2 to 3 hours so flavors will blend. Stir before serving. *Makes 4 servings*

Favorite recipe from *USA Rice*

# Jalapeño Coleslaw

6 cups shredded cabbage or coleslaw mix
2 tomatoes, seeded and chopped
6 green onions, coarsely chopped
2 jalapeño peppers,* finely chopped**
¼ cup cider vinegar
3 tablespoons honey
1 teaspoon salt

*Jalapeño peppers can sting and irritate the skin, so wear rubber gloves when handling peppers and do not touch your eyes.*

**For a milder coleslaw, discard seeds and veins when chopping the jalapeños.*

**1.** Combine cabbage, tomatoes, green onions, jalapeños, vinegar, honey and salt in large serving bowl; mix well. Cover; refrigerate at least 2 hours.

**2.** Stir well before serving.                         *Makes 4 servings*

# Best-of-the-West Bean Salad

¾ cup PACE® Picante Sauce
2 tablespoons chopped fresh cilantro leaves
2 tablespoons red wine vinegar
1 tablespoon vegetable oil
1 large green pepper, diced (about 1 cup)
1 medium red onion, very thinly sliced (about ½ cup)
1 can (about 15 ounces) kidney beans, rinsed and drained
1 can (about 15 ounces) pinto beans, rinsed and drained

Stir the picante sauce, cilantro, vinegar, oil, pepper, onion, kidney beans and pinto beans in a medium bowl. Cover and refrigerate for 2 hours, stirring occasionally during chilling time. Garnish with additional cilantro.                         *Makes 8 servings*

**Prep Time:** 10 minutes • **Chill Time:** 2 hours

★Jalapeño Coleslaw★

# Grilled Potato Salad

**Dressing**
  4 tablespoons country-style Dijon mustard
  1 tablespoon white wine or apple cider vinegar
  3 tablespoons olive oil
  2 tablespoons chopped fresh dill
  ½ teaspoon salt
  ¼ teaspoon black pepper

**Salad**
  1 teaspoon salt
  2 pounds small red potatoes
  2 tablespoons olive oil
  1 green onion, thinly sliced

**1.** Combine all dressing ingredients in glass measuring cup; stir well. Set aside.

**2.** Bring 8 cups water and 1 teaspoon salt to a boil in large saucepan over medium-high heat. Cut potatoes into ½-inch slices. Add potatoes to water; boil 5 minutes. Drain; return potatoes to saucepan. Drizzle with 2 tablespoons oil; toss lightly.

**3.** Prepare grill for direct cooking. Spray 1 side of large sheet of foil with nonstick cooking spray. Transfer potatoes to foil; fold into packet. Place potato packet on grid over medium-high heat. Grill 10 minutes or until potatoes are tender. Transfer potatoes to serving bowl. Sprinkle with green onion. Toss gently with reserved dressing. Serve warm.

*Makes 4 servings*

# Sassy Cowgirl Sweets

## Wacky Watermelon

4 cups diced seedless watermelon (1-inch cubes)
¼ cup strawberry fruit spread
2 cups vanilla frozen yogurt
2 tablespoons mini chocolate chips, divided

**1.** Place 2 cups watermelon and fruit spread in blender; pulse on low until smooth. Add remaining 2 cups watermelon; pulse until smooth. Add frozen yogurt, 1 cup at a time, pulsing until smooth after each addition.

**2.** Pour mixture into 8×4-inch loaf pan; freeze 2 hours or until mixture begins to harden around edge of pan. Stir well until mixture is smooth and slushy. Stir in 1 tablespoon plus 1½ teaspoons chocolate chips. Smooth top of mixture with back of spoon. Sprinkle evenly with remaining 1½ teaspoons chocolate chips. Cover pan with foil; freeze 6 hours or overnight.

**3.** To serve, place pan in warm water briefly; invert onto cutting board. Let stand 5 minutes on cutting board to soften slightly. Cut loaf into slices. Serve immediately.

**4.** Wrap any leftover slices individually in plastic wrap and place upright in clean loaf pan. Store in freezer. *Makes 12 servings*

# Fresh Berry-Berry Cobbler

¼ cup sugar

1 teaspoon cornstarch

12 ounces fresh raspberries

8 ounces fresh blueberries

¼ cup CREAM OF WHEAT® Hot Cereal (Instant, 1-minute,
2½-minute or 10-minute cook time), uncooked

¼ cup all-purpose flour

¼ cup ground almonds

2 teaspoons baking powder

¼ teaspoon salt

¼ cup (½ stick) butter, cut into small pieces, softened

¼ cup milk

1 egg

1 tablespoon sugar

Ice cream or whipped cream (optional)

**1.** Preheat oven to 450°F. Blend sugar and cornstarch in mixing bowl. Add berries and toss to coat. Pour into 8-inch square baking pan; set aside.

**2.** Combine Cream of Wheat, flour, almonds, baking powder and salt in food processor. Add butter; pulse several times until well combined. Add milk and egg; pulse until mixed thoroughly. Spread evenly over fruit mixture. Sprinkle sugar over top.

**3.** Bake 20 minutes. Let stand 5 minutes before serving. Serve in shallow bowls with ice cream or whipped cream, if desired. *Makes 6 servings*

**Tip:** For an elegant presentation, serve in a martini glass and top with a fresh sprig of mint.

**Prep Time:** 10 minutes • **Start to Finish Time:** 35 minutes

# Texas Sheet Cake

2 cups all-purpose flour
⅔ cup unsweetened cocoa powder
1¼ teaspoons baking soda
1 teaspoon salt
¼ teaspoon baking powder
1 cup granulated sugar
¾ cup (1½ sticks) butter, softened
⅔ cup packed brown sugar
3 eggs
1 teaspoon vanilla
1⅓ cups water
　Prepared chocolate frosting
　Chopped pecans (optional)

**1.** Preheat oven to 350°F. Grease 13×9-inch baking pan.

**2.** Combine flour, cocoa, baking soda, salt and baking powder in medium bowl. Beat granulated sugar, butter and brown sugar in large bowl with electric mixer at medium-high speed 2 minutes or until light and creamy. Add eggs and vanilla; beat 2 minutes. Add flour mixture alternately with water; beat just until blended. Pour batter into prepared pan.

**3.** Bake 25 to 35 minutes or until toothpick inserted into center comes out clean. Frost hot cake with chocolate frosting. Top with pecans, if desired. Cool in pan on wire rack. *Makes about 16 servings*

## TIP

Texas Sheet Cake is a basic chocolate cake that's loved by all. It's simply a classic, so it's a good recipe to whip up in a short amount of time for any occasion. Traditionally, pecans are sprinkled on top or added to the frosting, but walnuts may be used instead.

# Uncle Sam's Hat

1 package (18 ounces) refrigerated chocolate chip cookie dough
2 cups powdered sugar
2 to 4 tablespoons milk
   Red and blue food coloring

**1.** Preheat oven to 350°F. Lightly grease 12-inch round pizza pan and cookie sheet. Press dough evenly onto prepared pizza pan; cut into hat shape as shown in photo. Press scraps together and flatten heaping tablespoons of dough on prepared cookie sheet. Using 1½- to 2-inch star cookie cutter, cut out 3 stars; remove and discard dough scraps.

**2.** Bake stars 5 to 7 minutes and hat 7 to 9 minutes or until lightly browned at edges. Cool stars 1 minute on cookie sheet. Remove stars to wire rack; cool completely. Cool hat completely in pan on rack.

**3.** Combine powdered sugar and milk, 1 tablespoon at a time, to make medium-thick pourable glaze. Spread small amount of glaze over stars and place on waxed paper; let stand until glaze is set. Tint half of glaze red, tint one quarter of glaze blue and leave remaining quarter of glaze white.

**4.** Decorate hat with red, white and blue glazes as shown in photo; arrange stars on blue band of hat. Let stand until glaze is set.

*Makes 1 large cookie*

# Lemon-Lime Daiquiri Layered Dessert

2 cups lime sherbet, softened
1 package (8 ounces) PHILADELPHIA® Cream Cheese Spread
1 can (14 ounces) sweetened condensed milk
½ cup lemon juice
1 tub (8 ounces) COOL WHIP® Whipped Topping, thawed

**LINE** 9×5-inch loaf pan with foil. Spoon sherbet into prepared pan; spread to form even layer in pan. Freeze 10 minutes.

*continued on page 116*

*Lemon-Lime Daiquiri Layered Dessert, continued*

**BEAT** cream cheese spread in large bowl with wire whisk until creamy. Gradually add sweetened condensed milk and lemon juice, beating until well blended. Stir in whipped topping; spread over sherbet layer in pan.

**FREEZE** at least 3 hours or overnight. Invert loaf onto a serving plate and remove foil. Garnish with lemon and lime slices, if desired. Cut into 12 slices to serve. Store leftover dessert in freezer.      *Makes 12 servings.*

**Prep Time:** 15 minutes • **Total Time:** 3 hours 25 minutes (includes freezing)

# Easy Pineapple Citrus Layered Cake

1 (14- to 16-ounce) frozen prepared pound cake, thawed
1 package (8 ounces) cream cheese, softened
1 cup powdered sugar
1 tablespoon grated orange peel
1 tablespoon orange juice
¾ teaspoon almond or vanilla extract
1 can (20 ounces) DOLE® Crushed Pineapple, well drained
  Sliced almonds, toasted (optional)

• Slice pound cake horizontally into thirds; set aside.

• Beat together cream cheese, sugar, orange peel, orange juice and almond extract in large bowl until smooth and blended. Stir in pineapple.

• Place bottom cake layer on serving platter, spread with one-third of pineapple mixture over cake. Repeat layers, ending with pineapple mixture. Chill at least 1 hour or overnight before serving. Sprinkle with almonds, if desired.      *Makes 10 servings*

**Prep Time:** 20 minutes • **Chill Time:** 1 hour

# Margarita Cupcakes

1 package (about 18 ounces) white cake mix
¾ cup plus 2 tablespoons margarita mix, divided
2 eggs
⅓ cup vegetable oil
¼ cup water
3 teaspoons grated lime peel, divided (about 3 limes)
  Juice of 1 lime
2 tablespoons tequila or lime juice
3 cups powdered sugar
1 tablespoon sparkling or granulated sugar
1 tablespoon salt (optional)
  Green and yellow food coloring
  Lime peel strips (optional)

**1.** Preheat oven to 350°F. Line 24 standard (2½-inch) muffin cups with paper baking cups.

**2.** Combine cake mix, ¾ cup margarita mix, eggs, oil, water, 1 teaspoon lime peel and lime juice in large bowl. Whisk 2 minutes or until well blended. Spoon batter evenly into prepared cups.

**3.** Bake 20 to 25 minutes or until toothpick inserted into centers comes out clean. Remove cupcakes to wire racks; cool completely.

**4.** Combine tequila, remaining 2 tablespoons margarita mix and 2 teaspoons lime peel in medium bowl. Gradually whisk in powdered sugar until desired consistency is reached. Combine sparkling sugar and salt, if desired, in small bowl. Add food coloring, one drop at a time, until desired shade of green is reached.

**5.** Spread glaze over cupcakes; dip edges in sugar-salt mixture. Garnish with lime peel strips. *Makes 24 cupcakes*

# Easy Peach Cobbler

8 cups peeled and sliced peaches, nectarines or apples
   (½-inch-thick slices)
1 cup granulated sugar
⅔ cup plus 2 tablespoons BISQUICK®, divided
1 teaspoon ground cinnamon
2 tablespoons firmly packed brown sugar
¼ cup (½ stick) I CAN'T BELIEVE IT'S NOT BUTTER!® Spread
2 tablespoons milk

Preheat oven to 400°F.

In large bowl, combine peaches, granulated sugar, 2 tablespoons baking mix and cinnamon. In 11×7-inch baking dish, arrange peach mixture; set aside.

In medium bowl, mix remaining ⅔ cup baking mix with brown sugar. With pastry blender or 2 knives, cut in I Can't Believe It's Not Butter!® Spread until mixture is size of small peas. Stir in milk just until moistened. Drop by teaspoonfuls onto peach mixture.

Bake 30 minutes or until peaches are tender and topping is golden. Let stand 5 minutes before serving. Serve warm and, if desired, with vanilla ice cream. *Makes 6 servings*

**Prep Time:** 15 minutes • **Cook Time:** 30 minutes

# Tres Leches Cake

1 package (about 18 ounces) white cake mix, plus ingredients
   to prepare mix
1 can (14 ounces) sweetened condensed milk
1 cup milk
1 cup whipping cream
1 container (8 ounces) whipped topping, thawed
   Fresh fruit (optional)

**1.** Preheat oven to 350°F. Spray 13×9-inch baking pan with nonstick cooking spray.

**2.** Prepare cake mix according to package directions. Pour batter into prepared pan. Bake 35 to 40 minutes or until toothpick inserted into center comes out clean. Cool in pan 5 minutes.

**3.** Meanwhile, combine condensed milk, milk and whipping cream in 4-cup measure. Poke holes all over warm cake with wooden skewer or toothpick. Slowly pour milk mixture evenly over top of cake. Let cake stand 10 to 15 minutes to absorb liquid. Cover and refrigerate at least 1 hour.

**4.** Spread whipped topping over cake. Garnish with fruit. Keep cake covered and refrigerated.                        *Makes 12 to 15 servings*

**TIP**

Tres Leches, meaning three milks, is a very popular dessert in Latin America, traditionally made with evaporated milk, condensed milk and heavy cream. Allowing the cake to fully absorb the milk mixture gives it a moist yet light consistency. Try sprinkling flaked coconut over the topping for a delicious tropical flair.

# Acknowledgments

The publisher would like to thank the companies listed below for the use of their recipes and photos in this publication.

Courtesy The Beef Checkoff

Campbell Soup Company

Cream of Wheat® Cereal

Dole Food Company, Inc.

Grandma's®, A Division of B&G Foods, Inc.

VELVEETA is a registered trademark of Kraft Foods

Ortega®, A Division of B&G Foods, Inc.

Reckitt Benckiser Inc.

Unilever

USA Rice Federation®

**A**
All-American Onion Burger, 34
**B**
Barbecue Chicken Sliders, 16
Barbequed Ribs, 46
BBQ Beef Sandwiches, 38
**Beans**
Best-of-the-West Bean Salad, 104
Campfire Hot Dogs, 28
Charred Corn Salad, 98
Cowboy Coffee Chili, 48
Hot and Spicy Hummus Dip, 16
Layered Beer Bean Dip, 6
Mama's Best Baked Beans, 102
Santa Fe Salad, 102
Smokin' Texas Chili, 44
Tex-Mex Toasts, 8
Tijuana T-Bones, 40
**Beer**
Chicken Wings in Cerveza, 86
Grilled Chicken with Chili Beer Baste, 78
Grilled Skirt Steak Fajitas, 30
Layered Beer Bean Dip, 6
Pulled Pork Sandwiches, 62
Rio Grande Ribs, 60
Texas Smoked BBQ Brisket, 24
**Bell Peppers**
Best-of-the-West Bean Salad, 104
Chili-Rubbed Grilled Vegetable Kabobs, 92
Grilled Skirt Steak Fajitas, 30
Puerco Sabrosas (Savory Pork), 58
Texas Chili, 32
Best 'Cue Coleslaw, 96
Best-of-the-West Bean Salad, 104
Bodacious Grilled Ribs, 66
Bold and Zesty Beef Back Ribs, 42
**C**
**Cakes**
Easy Pineapple Citrus Layered Cake, 116
Margarita Cupcakes, 118
Texas Sheet Cake, 112
Tres Leches Cake, 122

California Burger, 34
Campfire Hot Dogs, 28
Cavemen Beef Back Ribs, 20
Charred Corn Salad, 98
Chicken Wings in Cerveza, 86
Chicken with Grilled Pineapple Salsa, 76
Chili Burger, 34
Chili con Queso, 8
Chili-Rubbed Grilled Vegetable Kabobs, 92
Chipotle-Rubbed Flank Steak, 36
Classic Baby Back Ribs, 64
**Corn**
Charred Corn Salad, 98
Chili-Rubbed Grilled Vegetable Kabobs, 92
Easy Taco Dip, 12
Salsa-Buttered Corn on the Cob, 100
Santa Fe Salad, 102
Super-Moist Cornbread, 94
Velveeta® Southwestern Corn Dip, 18
Cowboy Coffee Chili, 48
Cumin BBQ Chicken, 72
**D**
**Dips**
Chili con Queso, 8
Easy Taco Dip, 12
Hot and Spicy Hummus Dip, 16
Layered Beer Bean Dip, 6
Velveeta® Southwestern Corn Dip, 18
**E**
Easy Peach Cobbler, 120
Easy Pineapple Citrus Layered Cake, 116
Easy Taco Dip, 12
Enchilada Slow-Roasted Baby Back Ribs, 50
**F**
Fresh Berry-Berry Cobbler, 110
**Frozen Desserts**
Lemon-Lime Daiquiri Layered Dessert, 114
Wacky Watermelon, 108

# Index

## G

Galveston Shrimp Salad, 10
Garlicky Gilroy Chicken Wings, 74
Grilled Chicken with Chili Beer
  Baste, 78
Grilled Chicken with Southern
  Barbecue Sauce, 82
Grilled Chipotle Chicken
  Sandwiches, 84
Grilled Picante BBQ Chicken, 86
Grilled Potato Salad, 106
Grilled Skirt Steak Fajitas, 30
Grilled T-Bone Steaks with BBQ
  Rub, 43
**Grilling Recipes**
  All-American Onion Burger, 34
  Baby Back Ribs, 64
  Barbequed Ribs, 46
  Bodacious Grilled Ribs, 66
  Bold and Zesty Beef Back Ribs, 42
  California Burger, 34
  Cavemen Beef Back Ribs, 20
  Chicken with Grilled Pineapple
    Salsa, 76
  Chili Burger, 34
  Chili-Rubbed Grilled Vegetable
    Kabobs, 92
  Chipotle-Rubbed Flank Steak, 36
  Cumin BBQ Chicken, 72
  Grilled Chicken with Chili Beer
    Baste, 78
  Grilled Chicken with Southern
    Barbecue Sauce, 82
  Grilled Chipotle Chicken
    Sandwiches, 84
  Grilled Picante BBQ Chicken, 86
  Grilled Potato Salad, 106
  Grilled Skirt Steak Fajitas, 30
  Grilled T-Bone Steaks with BBQ
    Rub, 43
  Luscious Oniony Cheeseburger, 34
  Pizza Burger, 34
  Pork Tenderloin Sliders, 54
  Rustic Texas-Que Pizza, 14
  Salisbury Steak Burger, 34
  Santa Fe BBQ Ranch Salad, 90

Spicy Baby Back Ribs, 70
Spicy Smoked Beef Ribs, 26
Tangy Western Burger, 34
Texas Barbecued Ribs, 52
Texas Meets N.Y. Strip Steaks, 28
Texas Smoked BBQ Brisket, 24
Tijuana T-Bones, 40

## H

Hot and Spicy Hummus Dip, 16

## J

Jalapeño Coleslaw, 104

## L

Layered Beer Bean Dip, 6
Lemon-Lime Daiquiri Layered
  Dessert, 114
Luscious Oniony Cheeseburger, 34

## M

Mama's Best Baked Beans, 102
Margarita Cupcakes, 118

## P

Pizza Burger, 34
Pork Paint, 64
Pork Tenderloin Sliders, 54
**Potatoes**: Grilled Potato Salad, 106
Puerco Sabrosas (Savory Pork), 58
Pulled Pork Sandwiches, 62
Pulled Turkey Sandwiches, 88

## R

**Ribs**
  Baby Back Ribs, 64
  Barbequed Ribs, 46
  Bodacious Grilled Ribs, 66
  Bold and Zesty Beef Back Ribs, 42
  Cavemen Beef Back Ribs, 20
  Enchilada Slow-Roasted Baby
    Back Ribs, 50
  Rio Grande Ribs, 60
  Spicy Baby Back Ribs, 70
  Spicy Smoked Beef Ribs, 26
  Sweet 'n' Sour Country Ribs, 56
  Texas Barbecued Ribs, 52
Rio Grande Ribs, 60
Rough-Cut Smoky Red Pork, 68
Rustic Texas-Que Pizza, 14

## S

**Salads**
- Best 'Cue Coleslaw, 96
- Best-of-the-West Bean Salad, 104
- Charred Corn Salad, 98
- Galveston Shrimp Salad, 10
- Grilled Potato Salad, 106
- Jalapeño Coleslaw, 104
- Santa Fe BBQ Ranch Salad, 90
- Santa Fe Salad, 102

Salisbury Steak Burger, 34
Salsa-Buttered Corn on the Cob, 100

**Sandwiches**
- All-American Onion Burger, 34
- Barbecue Chicken Sliders, 16
- BBQ Beef Sandwiches, 38
- California Burger, 34
- Campfire Hot Dogs, 28
- Chili Burger, 34
- Grilled Chipotle Chicken Sandwiches, 84
- Luscious Oniony Cheeseburger, 34
- Pizza Burger, 34
- Pork Tenderloin Sliders, 54
- Pulled Pork Sandwiches, 62
- Pulled Turkey Sandwiches, 88
- Salisbury Steak Burger, 34
- Shredded BBQ Chicken Sandwiches, 80
- Slow-Cooked Mini Pulled Pork Bites, 4
- Spicy Onion Steak Sandwiches, 22
- Tangy Western Burger, 34

Santa Fe BBQ Ranch Salad, 90
Santa Fe Salad, 102
Sausage and Cheddar Cornbread, 100
Shredded BBQ Chicken Sandwiches, 80

**Shrimp**: Galveston Shrimp Salad, 10

**Slow Cooker Recipes**
- BBQ Beef Sandwiches, 38
- Easy Taco Dip, 12
- Mama's Best Baked Beans, 102
- Rio Grande Ribs, 60

Rough-Cut Smoky Red Pork, 68
Slow-Cooked Mini Pulled Pork Bites, 4
Slow-Cooked Mini Pulled Pork Bites, 4
Smokin' Texas Chili, 44
Spicy Baby Back Ribs, 70
Spicy Onion Steak Sandwiches, 22
Spicy Sausage Mac & Cheese Bake, 94
Spicy Smoked Beef Ribs, 26
Super-Moist Cornbread, 94
Sweet 'n' Sour Country Ribs, 56

**Sweet Potatoes**: Sweet 'n' Sour Country Ribs, 56

## T

Tangy Western Burger, 34
Texas Barbecued Ribs, 52
Texas Chili, 32
Texas Meets N.Y. Strip Steaks, 28
Texas Sheet Cake, 112
Texas Smoked BBQ Brisket, 24
Tex-Mex Toasts, 8
Tijuana T-Bones, 40

**Tomatoes, Fresh**
- Galveston Shrimp Salad, 10
- Grilled Skirt Steak Fajitas, 30
- Jalapeño Coleslaw, 104
- Rustic Texas-Que Pizza, 14
- Santa Fe BBQ Ranch Salad, 90

Tres Leches Cake, 122

**Turkey**: Pulled Turkey Sandwiches, 88

20 Minute Marinade, 56

## U

Uncle Sam's Hat, 114

## V

Velveeta® Southwestern Corn Dip, 18

## W

Wacky Watermelon, 108

# METRIC CONVERSION CHART

## VOLUME MEASUREMENTS (dry)

$1/8$ teaspoon = 0.5 mL
$1/4$ teaspoon = 1 mL
$1/2$ teaspoon = 2 mL
$3/4$ teaspoon = 4 mL
1 teaspoon = 5 mL
1 tablespoon = 15 mL
2 tablespoons = 30 mL
$1/4$ cup = 60 mL
$1/3$ cup = 75 mL
$1/2$ cup = 125 mL
$2/3$ cup = 150 mL
$3/4$ cup = 175 mL
1 cup = 250 mL
2 cups = 1 pint = 500 mL
3 cups = 750 mL
4 cups = 1 quart = 1 L

## VOLUME MEASUREMENTS (fluid)

1 fluid ounce (2 tablespoons) = 30 mL
4 fluid ounces ($1/2$ cup) = 125 mL
8 fluid ounces (1 cup) = 250 mL
12 fluid ounces ($1 1/2$ cups) = 375 mL
16 fluid ounces (2 cups) = 500 mL

## WEIGHTS (mass)

$1/2$ ounce = 15 g
1 ounce = 30 g
3 ounces = 90 g
4 ounces = 120 g
8 ounces = 225 g
10 ounces = 285 g
12 ounces = 360 g
16 ounces = 1 pound = 450 g

## DIMENSIONS

$1/16$ inch = 2 mm
$1/8$ inch = 3 mm
$1/4$ inch = 6 mm
$1/2$ inch = 1.5 cm
$3/4$ inch = 2 cm
1 inch = 2.5 cm

## OVEN TEMPERATURES

250°F = 120°C
275°F = 140°C
300°F = 150°C
325°F = 160°C
350°F = 180°C
375°F = 190°C
400°F = 200°C
425°F = 220°C
450°F = 230°C

## BAKING PAN SIZES

| Utensil | Size in Inches/Quarts | Metric Volume | Size in Centimeters |
|---|---|---|---|
| Baking or Cake Pan (square or rectangular) | $8 \times 8 \times 2$ | 2 L | $20 \times 20 \times 5$ |
| | $9 \times 9 \times 2$ | 2.5 L | $23 \times 23 \times 5$ |
| | $12 \times 8 \times 2$ | 3 L | $30 \times 20 \times 5$ |
| | $13 \times 9 \times 2$ | 3.5 L | $33 \times 23 \times 5$ |
| Loaf Pan | $8 \times 4 \times 3$ | 1.5 L | $20 \times 10 \times 7$ |
| | $9 \times 5 \times 3$ | 2 L | $23 \times 13 \times 7$ |
| Round Layer Cake Pan | $8 \times 1 1/2$ | 1.2 L | $20 \times 4$ |
| | $9 \times 1 1/2$ | 1.5 L | $23 \times 4$ |
| Pie Plate | $8 \times 1 1/4$ | 750 mL | $20 \times 3$ |
| | $9 \times 1 1/4$ | 1 L | $23 \times 3$ |
| Baking Dish or Casserole | 1 quart | 1 L | — |
| | $1 1/2$ quart | 1.5 L | — |
| | 2 quart | 2 L | — |